I Can COOK!

Lynette Baxter

ARMADILLO

Contents

Safe cooking

Kitchens can be dangerous places, so it's very important that you read these safety tips before you start cooking.

1 ALWAYS HAVE A GROWN-UP WITH YOU

Before you begin, show him or her what you plan to do and where you might need some help. Read all the way through the recipe to make sure you have all the ingredients and equipment you need before you start.

2 PROTECT YOURSELF!

Unless you are wearing something old, put on an apron to protect your clothes. Tie back your hair if it's long and take off jewellery, watches, trailing scarves and ties.

3 BE CAREFUL ABOUT HYGIENE

People are going to eat what you cook! Always wash your hands before you start and between handling different kinds of foods. Make sure all surfaces and utensils are clean. Keep pets out of the kitchen.

4 TAKE CARE WITH HOT STOVES AND PANS

Always use oven gloves to handle hot things. Remember that hobs, ovens and pans can stay hot long after you have finished with them. Switch electrical equipment off as soon as it is no longer needed.

5 KEEP SMALL CHILDREN OUT

Little ones may not understand the dangers as well as you do.

6 CLEAN UP AS YOU GO

Clear spills up at once so that you don't slip in them. Make sure you leave the kitchen as tidy as you found it.

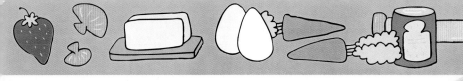

Pizza toasts

Making pizzas is fun because you can choose whatever toppings you like — even sweet ones. This recipe makes a quick and easy pizza snack.

FOR 2 PEOPLE

You will need
- ★ 2 thick slices of bread or 2 crumpets, or a plain muffin, or a large bap cut in half to make 2 slices, or a baguette cut into halves or thirds and then sliced lengthways
- ★ 2 large tomatoes, sliced thinly
- ★ 100g grated cheddar cheese or sliced mozzarella cheese
- ★ salt and pepper
- ★ dried oregano
- ★ any toppings you like as long as they are already cooked or can be eaten raw, such as flaked tuna, chopped ham, cooked prawns, cooked mushrooms, or sliced peppers

1 Place your chosen pizza base under a hot grill, bottom side up. Toast it until crispy. Carefully take it out and turn it the other way up. Turn the grill down to a low/medium heat.

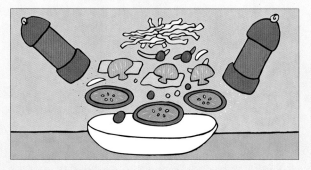

2 Cover the base with a layer of tomato slices. Sprinkle on some salt, pepper and oregano. Add your favourite toppings and cover with cheese.

3 Return the pizzas to the grill and cook until the cheese bubbles and browns. Doing this slowly on a low heat will allow the other ingredients to heat through while the cheese is cooking.

Fruit smoothies

Smoothies make a super snack or a healthy breakfast. This recipe uses raspberries, but any soft fruit, such as strawberries, blueberries, peaches, apricots, or mangoes will work. Banana makes the drink rich and thick.

MAKES 4 SMALL OR 2 LARGE GLASSES

You will need
★ 250g raspberries
★ 1 ripe banana
★ 250g natural yogurt
★ 300ml whole or semi-skimmed milk

1 This couldn't be easier! Chop the banana into slices and place it in a blender or food processor with all the other ingredients. If you are using larger fruits with stones, take these out first. Process until smooth.

2 If the smoothie is too thick, add a little more milk. You can add a little honey to sweeten it if you think it's necessary. You could also try making this with frozen fruits for a slushier drink on a hot day.

Carrot and coriander soup

This soup is easy to make. You can use the same method to turn almost any vegetable into steaming soup.

SERVES 2–3

You will need
★ 45ml vegetable oil
★ 4 large carrots, peeled and roughly sliced
★ 1 small potato (about 100g), peeled and roughly chopped
★ 1 onion, peeled and roughly chopped
★ 10–15ml ground coriander
★ 600ml vegetable stock
★ salt and pepper

1 Heat the oil in a large saucepan over a medium/high heat. Add the vegetables and ground coriander and cook for 5 minutes, stirring from time to time.

2 Add the stock, bring to the boil and then simmer until the vegetables feel soft when you poke them with a sharp knife. This should take about 20 minutes.

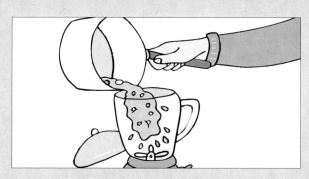

3 Very carefully pour the mixture into a blender or food processor and whizz until smooth. You may have to do this in two batches, making sure you get a mix of vegetables and liquid in each batch.

4 Return the soup to the saucepan and warm it over a low heat. Add salt and pepper to taste and carefully pour it into bowls. You could add some herb leaves for a finishing touch if you like.

Cheesy pinwheels

These are delicious cold, but even better served warm, either just after baking or gently reheated. They are ideal to serve at a party.

MAKES ABOUT 24

You will need
★ 375g packet ready-rolled puff pastry, defrosted if frozen
★ 150g mature Cheddar cheese, grated
★ 15–30ml yeast extract or mustard

1 Take the pastry out of the fridge about an hour before you use it so it will unroll without cracking. Preheat the oven to 200°C/400°F/Gas 6.

2 Lay the pastry flat on a clean worktop. Press it back together if it does crack a bit.

3 Thinly spread the yeast extract or mustard over the pastry, leaving a 2cm border along one short end. Don't worry if it looks uneven.

4 Sprinkle cheese evenly over the flavouring and press it down gently. Brush the uncovered strip with water. Roll up the pastry, starting at the opposite edge to the dampened strip. Press gently when you reach this strip to help it stick together.

5 Cut the roll into slices about 8–10mm wide and arrange these on baking trays, leaving 20–30mm between them to allow for spreading.

6 Bake for 10–12 minutes, until golden brown. Carefully transfer each pinwheel to a cooling rack, using a palette knife.

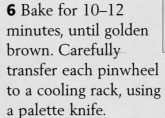

Savoury beans

Baked beans are good, but this recipe makes them even better. They would be great in a baked potato or with sausages or any other meat from the barbecue.

SERVES 2 AS A SNACK OR 4 AS A SIDE DISH

You will need
- ★ 415g can baked beans
- ★ 227g can chopped tomatoes
- ★ 4 rashers of rindless streaky bacon
- ★ 1 small onion, finely chopped
- ★ 15ml vegetable oil
- ★ dash of Worcestershire sauce or Tabasco (if you like)

1 Cut the bacon into bite-sized pieces. It's often easiest to use scissors for this.

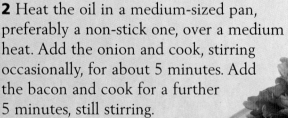

2 Heat the oil in a medium-sized pan, preferably a non-stick one, over a medium heat. Add the onion and cook, stirring occasionally, for about 5 minutes. Add the bacon and cook for a further 5 minutes, still stirring.

3 Add the beans and tomatoes and heat through, stirring all the time, until just beginning to bubble.

4 If you like, before serving add a shake of Worcestershire sauce for a little savoury spiciness. A couple of drops of Tabasco will give an even hotter and spicier result.

Omelettes

This is a great recipe to adapt for any occasion. You can fill the basic omelette with grated cheese, ham, sliced tomatoes ... whatever you like. Serve with crusty bread and a salad for an excellent lunch or supper dish.

SERVES 1

You will need
- ★ 3 large eggs
- ★ pinch of salt and pepper
- ★ 15ml cold water
- ★ 15ml chopped fresh herbs (optional)
- ★ 15ml vegetable oil

1 Carefully crack the eggs and drop the yolks and whites into a bowl. Don't drop any shell in! Add the salt, pepper, water and herbs if you are using them.

2 Use a fork to break up the eggs and whisk gently to make a smooth mixture.

3 Put the oil in a frying pan, preferably a non-stick one about 20cm across, and place over a medium/high heat. After about two minutes, carefully pour in the egg mixture.

4 Leave for one minute and then, using a palette knife or wooden spatula, pull the cooked egg away from the edge and allow the runny mixture to take its place. Keep doing this until the omelette is nearly set.

5 Carefully ease the palette knife under the omelette to loosen it and fold it in half. Slide it onto a plate and serve at once. A perfect omelette looks great, but it will taste just as good if the folding didn't work very well. It just takes practice.

Baked potatoes

You could cook your potato in a microwave oven, but to get a lovely fluffy middle with a crispy skin you really need to allow time and bake it in the oven. Buy potatoes that are good for baking — not too new or too small.

SERVES 4

You will need
★ 4 large, evenly-sized potatoes (about 200–250g each)
★ butter
★ fillings (see below)

1 Preheat the oven to 200°C/400°F/Gas 6.

2 Wash the potatoes. Place them on a baking tray and cut a large, deep cross in the top of each one.

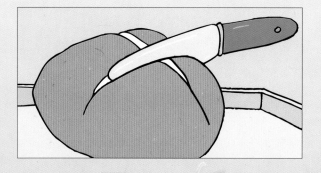

3 Cook the potatoes for 1¼ to 1½ hours until they feel soft all the way through when you push a sharp knife into the cross. Carefully take them out of the oven.

4 Protect your hands with a tea towel and squeeze each potato either side of the cross so that soft potato pushes up out of the slit. Push a piece of butter into the top if you wish and pile on the filling of your choice. Serve piping hot.

5 You could use savoury beans (page 8) or savoury mince (page 31) as hot fillings. Grated cheese, coleslaw, or tinned tuna mashed with mayonnaise make good cold fillings – or add your own favourite topping.

Sausage and mash

Here's a very popular meal — even in posh restaurants. Choose your favourite sausages from the huge range available now.

SERVES 4

You will need
★ 1 portion of mashed potatoes (see page 31)
★ about 500g of sausages

1 While the potatoes are cooking, you can grill or fry the sausages according to the instructions on the packet. Grilling is the healthiest option as you will lose some of the fat.

2 Mash the potatoes. You may like to flavour them as suggested on page 31.

3 Spoon the potatoes onto a serving dish and top with the sausages. You could serve this with savoury beans (page 8) for a really filling meal.

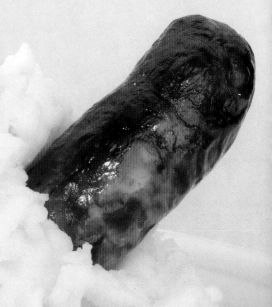

Cottage pie

This is real comfort food. You could add some cooked carrots or a handful of defrosted frozen peas to the mince … or both!

SERVES 4

You will need
★ **1 quantity savoury mince (see page 31)**
★ **1 quantity mashed potato (see page 31)**

1 Preheat the oven to 200°C/400°F/Gas 6.

2 Put the mince mixture in an ovenproof dish and allow it to cool.

3 Gently dollop spoonfuls of the potato over the mince.

4 With a spatula or a blunt knife, carefully spread the potato so it covers the mince and joins the edge of the dish. This should stop the gravy oozing over the potato as it cooks, but it's not a disaster if it does. You could mark the potato with a fork.

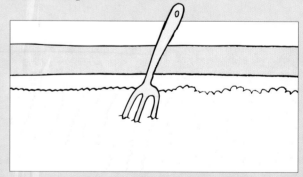

5 Place the dish on a baking tray (less messy if it boils over) and put it in the oven for 25–30 minutes until it is golden brown and piping hot.

Baked chicken parcels

The good thing about this recipe is that you can just multiply it to feed as many people as you need.

SERVES 1

You will need
- ★ 1 fresh chicken breast or leg joint
- ★ 2 mushrooms, thinly sliced
- ★ 2 thin slices of onion
- ★ 15ml lemon juice
- ★ salt and pepper
- ★ baking foil

1 Preheat the oven to 200°C/400°F/Gas 6.

2 Cut the foil to about 30cm square and lay it, shiny side down, on a work surface.

3 Place the chicken in the centre of the foil, top it with the mushrooms and onions, and add the lemon juice and a pinch of salt and pepper.

4 Pull up the sides and edges of the foil and twist them together at the top. The chicken should be sealed in, but not too tightly. Place the parcel on a baking tray in the oven for 35–40 minutes.

5 Remove the tray and very carefully open up the top of the foil. Return everything to the oven for 10 minutes to allow the chicken to brown a little.

6 Unwrap the foil on the serving plate so you serve up all the juices.

Spaghetti bolognese

Just about everybody loves spaghetti bolognese. If you are serving it to small children who might make a mess eating it, choose a different shape of pasta such as shells or twists. It will taste just as good.

SERVES 4

You will need
- ★ 1 quantity savoury mince (see page 31)
- ★ 400g can chopped tomatoes in juice
- ★ 15ml tomato purée
- ★ 5ml dried oregano
- ★ 400–500g dried pasta
- ★ grated cheese (preferably Parmesan)

1 Make up the mince as in the basic recipe on page 31 but replace the water with the canned tomatoes and add the tomato purée and oregano when you put in the stock cube.

2 Cook the pasta according to the directions on the packet.

3 Very carefully drain the cooked pasta in a colander or large sieve and dish it up onto plates or into bowls. Top with the bolognese sauce.

4 Let everyone sprinkle their own cheese on top. Parmesan is traditional, but you can use any cheese you enjoy.

Savoury rice

This is a really easy dish that you can vary as you like. A variation to make egg-fried rice is described at the end of the recipe below.

SERVES 4

You will need
★ 300–400g cooked rice (cook it yourself in advance or buy it ready cooked in pouches or frozen, defrosting before use)
★ 198g tin sweetcorn kernels, drained
★ 1 small onion, chopped finely
★ 15–30ml vegetable oil
★ 1 red or green pepper, seeded and chopped finely
★ 2 sticks celery, finely sliced
★ about 150g ham (not the wafer-thin type), roughly chopped

1 Heat the oil in a large frying pan over a medium heat.

2 Add the onion and cook for 5 minutes, stirring occasionally.

3 Add the pepper and celery and cook for a further 5 minutes.

4 Add the rice, sweetcorn and ham and cook for 5–10 minutes, stirring from time to time, until the mixture is piping hot. Now it's ready to serve!

5 To make egg-fried rice, whisk 2 eggs with 15ml soy sauce and pour this over the heated mixture while it is still in the pan. Keep stirring until the egg is set.

Banana icecream

It's hard to believe anything as easy as this can taste so good! Friends who are allergic to dairy products can also enjoy this treat.

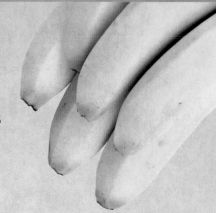

SERVES 4

You will need
★ 5 ripe but not squashy bananas

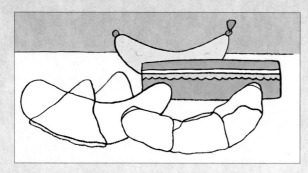

1 Peel the bananas, wrap each individually in clingfilm and place in a freezer overnight.

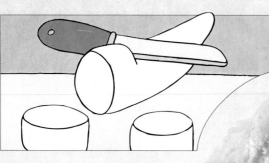

2 Remove the bananas from the freezer, leave them for 10 minutes, and then cut them into rough 5cm chunks. Be very careful when you are doing this.

3 Put the pieces of banana in a food processor and whizz. At first the mixture will look lumpy, but it soon becomes creamy.

4 This icecream is best served at once, but you could scrape the mixture into a plastic tub, cover it with a lid, and store it in the freezer.

5 You could serve this with any of the sauces and sprinkles on the next page – or just by itself.

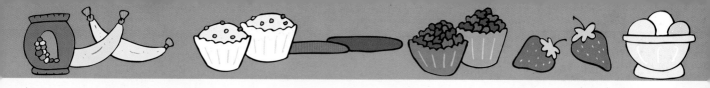

Sauces and sprinkles

Homemade sauces will make your icecream even more special, and they'd be just as good poured over simple sliced bananas.

Chocolate fudge sauce

MAKES ABOUT 300ML

You will need
★ 125ml whipping cream
★ 25g butter
★ 40g cocoa powder
★ 60g caster sugar
★ 60g soft brown sugar

Place all the ingredients in a small saucepan and stir them together over a low heat until they have melted and combined. Serve hot or cold.

Butterscotch sauce

MAKES ABOUT 300ML

You will need
★ 85g butter
★ 225g soft brown sugar
★ 200ml double cream

Put the butter and sugar in a saucepan over a medium heat until they are melted. Then bubble the mixture gently for five minutes. Carefully pour in the cream and heat through. Serve hot.

Sprinkles

You can buy all sorts of sprinkles specially designed for icecream, but you could also try some of these:

★ crushed chocolate-covered
  honyecomb bars
★ chocolate buttons
★ crushed flake bars
★ chopped nuts
★ dessicated coconut
★ candy-coated
  chocolate beans

Buns

If you need cakes in a hurry, buns are the answer. They take minutes to make and can be varied and decorated to suit the occasion.

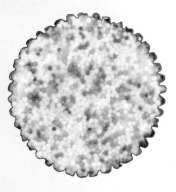

MAKES 12

You will need
★ 1 quantity sandwich cake mixture (see page 32)
★ bun cases and tins
★ 200g icing sugar and decorations if you wish

1 Preheat the oven to 190°C/375°F/ Gas 5. Arrange 12 bun cases in a bun tin.

2 Drop spoonfuls of the mixture into each bun case, trying to divide it evenly between the cases. There's no need to spread the mixture out in the cases.

3 Place the tray in the oven for about 20 minutes until the buns are risen and golden brown. Carefully transfer them to a cooling rack until they are cold.

4 Put the icing sugar in a bowl and add cold water 5ml (1 teaspoon) at a time until you have thick, smooth icing. For coloured icing, use a tiny drop of food colouring. Spread the icing on the buns, adding decorations if you wish.

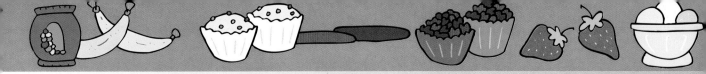

White chocolate fondue

You don't need a fondue set to make this delicious treat. Simply follow the directions for melting chocolate on page 32 and pour it into a pretty bowl to serve. Use a good brand of chocolate — not anything labelled as cooking chocolate.

SERVES 4

You will need
★ 300g white chocolate
★ 150ml double cream
★ 15–30ml orange juice
★ strawberries, sponge and chocolate finger biscuits, and/or marshmallows for dipping

1 Melt the chocolate as on page 32.

2 Stir in the cream and orange juice until just mixed. Reheat very carefully, stir again, and pour into a serving bowl. The fondue needs to be eaten straight away.

3 Sit the bowl on a large plate and surround it with the suggested dippers.

Chocolate crispies

These little cakes are so easy to make and simply delicious. You can add little marshmallows, raisins, cherries or nuts in place of some of the cornflakes if you like.

MAKES 12–15

You will need
★ **50g butter**
★ **60ml golden syrup**
★ **100g plain chocolate**
★ **75g cornflakes**
★ **bun cases and bun tins**

1 Place the butter, syrup and chocolate in a very large saucepan over a low heat. Stir until everything has melted together.

2 Very carefully take the pan off the heat and add the cornflakes. Stir gently until the flakes are evenly coated with the chocolate mixture.

3 Stand the bun cases in a bun tin to hold them steady. Put spoonfuls of the mixture into the bun cases. Try to leave the crispies to set before eating them!

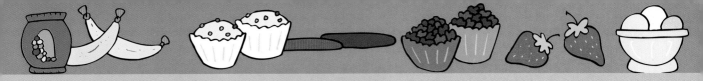

Crunchy mousse

Nobody who eats this mousse will be able to guess how easy it is to make. You could serve it with chocolate finger biscuits, as here, or by itself. Either way, it tastes wonderful!

SERVES 4

You will need
★ 2 average-sized chocolate honeycomb bars
★ 275ml double cream
★ 100ml thick natural yoghurt – Greek yoghurt would be good

1 Put the honeycomb bars in a large, clean plastic bag, hold the end closed and bang the bars with a wooden rolling pin or something similar until you have small chunks – stop before they become powder!

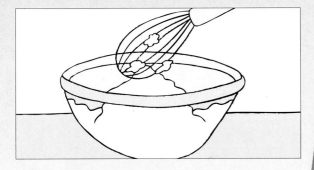

2 Place the cream in a large bowl and whisk it until the cream thickens and stands in peaks when you pull the whisk out. Gently mix the yoghurt into the cream.

3 Fold the crushed honeycomb bars into the cream and divide the mixture between 4 serving dishes.

4 Chill in the fridge for two hours before serving. During this time some of the honeycomb will start to melt and trickle through the mixture, while other pieces, protected by the chocolate, will stay crunchy. Delicious!

Flapjacks

Some of the easiest cakes to make are those where you simply melt the ingredients together. You could take out the coconut or add raisins or chocolate chips to this recipe if you prefer.

MAKES 20

You will need
* ★ 175g butter
* ★ 25g golden syrup
* ★ 125g soft brown sugar
* ★ 175g rolled porridge oats
* ★ 50g wholemeal plain flour
* ★ 50g desiccated coconut

1 Preheat the oven to 180°C/350°F/Gas 4. Grease a 28cm x 18cm swiss roll tin.

2 Place the butter and syrup in a large saucepan over a low heat and stir until they have melted together. Remove the pan from the heat.

3 Add the sugar, oats, flour and coconut, and mix well. Carefully turn the mixture into the tin and spread it out evenly.

4 Bake for 15 minutes, until golden.

5 Let the tin cool for 10 minutes, then mark the flapjack into squares or triangles. Be very careful. Everything will still be quite hot. When the flapjacks are still warm but not hot, remove them from the tin, using a palette knife to help you. Leave them on a rack to finish cooling.

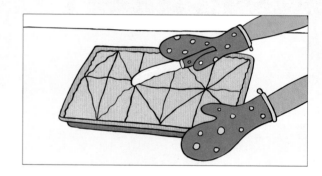

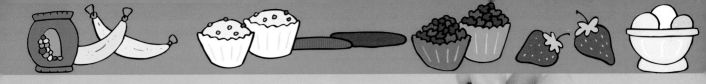

Fruit salad

**You can use any fruits you like in this recipe.
It might be fun to make a colour co-ordinated
salad — perhaps apricots, oranges, pineapple and
bananas, or apples, pears, kiwi fruit and green grapes.**

SERVES 4

You will need
★ 100ml orange juice
★ 75g golden syrup
★ small bunch of grapes
★ 1–2 satsumas
★ 1 apple
★ 1 pear
★ 100g strawberries with the green part
   removed
★ 1–2 bananas

1 Mix together the orange juice and syrup
until the syrup has dissolved.

2 Wash and dry all the fruit. Pull the
grapes from their stalks and put them in
a pretty bowl.

3 Peel the satsuma, divide it into segments,
and add them to the bowl.

4 Cut the apple and pear into quarters,
carefully cut out the core, and chop the
fruit into small pieces to add to the bowl.

5 Halve the strawberries and add them.

6 Add the banana, peeled and sliced.

7 Pour the orange syrup over the fruit and
mix very gently – clean hands do this best.
Keep the salad chilled until you serve it.

Breakfast pancakes

These little pancakes are delicious at any time of day but are a lovely treat for someone special for breakfast, specially when served with maple syrup and fresh fruit salad.

MAKES LOTS

You will need
- ★ 525g plain flour
- ★ 2.5ml bicarbonate of soda
- ★ 5ml cream of tartar
- ★ 10ml caster sugar
- ★ 1 egg
- ★ 285ml milk
- ★ vegetable oil
- ★ maple syrup – try to get the real thing rather than maple-flavoured syrup
- ★ fruit salad (page 23)

1 Sieve the flour, bicarbonate of soda and cream of tartar into a large bowl. Stir in the sugar.

2 Beat the egg and milk together and then slowly mix them into the flour mixture with a whisk, to make a smooth, thick batter.

3 Heat 15ml of oil in a frying pan over a medium/high heat. Add dessertspoonfuls of the mixture – you'll be able to cook several at a time – allowing space for them to spread.

4 When you see bubbles on the surface, flip the pancakes over with a palette knife and brown the base. Carefully lift the cooked pancakes out of the pan and place them on a plate. Keep them warm in a very low oven while you cook the rest.

5 Serve the plate of pancakes with a bowl of fruit salad and a jug of maple syrup.

Celebration cake

There are so many excuses to have a party that it's always useful to have this recipe up your sleeve. You can decorate the cake any way you like, remembering to leave room for candles if necessary!

MAKES ONE 20CM CAKE

You will need
★ 2 x sandwich cake recipe (see page 32)
★ 25g cocoa powder
★ chocolate or chocolate and hazelnut spread
★ chocolate buttons, sweets, etc. to decorate

1 Preheat the oven to 190°C/375°F/Gas 5. Grease two 20cm round sandwich tins and line the bases with greaseproof paper.

2 Make up the sandwich cake recipe as on page 32, but replace 25g of the flour with 25g cocoa powder. Sieve it in with the flour as cocoa powder is always lumpy.

3 Divide the mixture evenly between the tins and level the tops. Bake for 20–25 minutes until well risen. The cake should spring back when you press the middle gently with your finger.

4 Carefully run a palette knife around the edges of the cakes and turn them onto cooling racks. Leave them until completely cold.

5 Place one cake on a large plate, spread it generously with chocolate spread, and top it with the other cake. Cover this with a thick layer of spread, too.

6 Decorate as you like. Candy-coated sweets are great for spelling out names and messages.

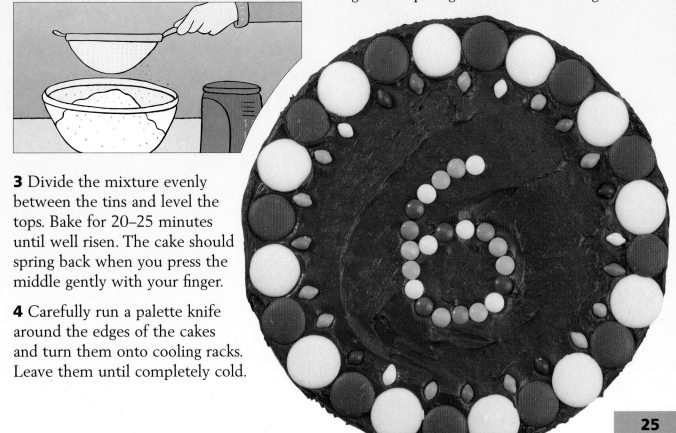

Fruit punch

This is a very useful recipe to have in your collection. It is delicious on a summer's day and ideal for parties. Lots of adults prefer a non-alcoholic drink too, especially if they are driving.

MAKES 2 LITRES

You will need
★ 600ml orange juice, chilled
★ 300ml pineapple juice, chilled
★ juice of 1 lemon
★ 100g caster sugar
★ 1 litre ginger ale, chilled
★ icecubes

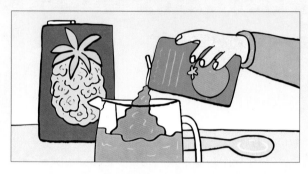

1 Mix the fruit juices in a large jug.

2 Add the sugar and stir until dissolved. You will need a long spoon for this!

3 Just before serving, add the ginger ale and ice and mix again.

4 You could add some thin orange and lemon slices and perhaps some sprigs of mint to the jug if you like.

Cheese and carrot dip

Dips are always popular at parties or when you are simply chatting with friends. It's even nicer to serve one you have made yourself.

SERVES 4–6

You will need
- ★ 2 large carrots, peeled
- ★ 200g cheddar cheese
- ★ 100g mayonnaise
- ★ 30ml tomato ketchup
- ★ dippers (see below)

1 Coarsely grate the carrots and cheese and place them in a large bowl.

2 Add the mayonnaise and ketchup and mix everything together thoroughly. If the mixture seems too thick, you could stir in a little milk.

3 Spoon the mixture into a serving bowl and sit this on a large plate on which you can arrange your dippers. These could include carrot and celery sticks, potato chips, breadsticks, and your favourite savoury biscuits.

Chocolate-dipped fruit

These would make a lovely present or could be a light dessert after a heavy main course. They are best eaten the day they are made, but could be kept in the fridge overnight if necessary.

ADJUST QUANTITIES AS REQUIRED

You will need
★ melted plain and white chocolate
  (see page 32)
★ strawberries with the green stalk left on
★ green grapes
★ dried apricots (the no-need-to-soak variety)

1 Store all the fruit you are using in the fridge overnight. This will help the chocolate to set quickly.

2 First dip the fruit in the white chocolate, holding it at an angle. Gently shake off any excess chocolate and place the fruit on a tray lined with greaseproof paper. Repeat with all the fruit and leave them to set.

3 Now repeat the process with the plain chocolate, but angling the fruit the other way. With a little practice, you'll soon be able to do this, and the fruits will taste just as good if they look wobbly!

4 Put the double-dipped fruit back on the paper and chill until set and ready to eat.

Fast flans

By using a sheet of ready-rolled puff pastry, you can make and bake a stunning flan in less than half an hour. All sorts of sweet and savoury fillings will work, but it's best to use ready-cooked ones as the flan cooks very quickly.

SERVES 4–6

You will need
★ 375g packet ready-rolled puff pastry
  (about 350mm x 225mm)
★ fillings (see below)

1 Remove the pastry from the fridge about an hour before you want to use it, so that you can unroll it into a neat rectangle with no cracks.

2 Preheat the oven to 220°C/425°F/Gas 7.

3 Carefully unroll the pastry onto a large baking tray. With a sharp knife, score a border about 15mm inside the edge, trying not to cut all the way through.

4 Prick the centre of the pastry, but not the border, all over with a fork. The base is now ready for any number of fillings, which may be served hot or cold.

Savoury fillings: sliced tomatoes and grated cheddar cheese; fried mushrooms, sliced ham and grated cheddar cheese

Sweet fillings: tinned apricots and plums; cream cheese sprinkled with caster sugar and topped with strawberries or raspberries.

5 Bake the flan for 15 minutes or until the edges are risen, crisp and golden brown.

Useful things to know

Here are some very useful recipes and techniques that have been used more than once in the recipes in this book and will stand you in good stead when you are cooking.

How to work

All cooks have their own methods and short-cuts, but it is a good plan to work in the order suggested here until you have had lots of practice.

1 Before you do anything, read and follow the safety tips on page 3. They are really important.

2 Next read the recipe and check that you have all the ingredients and all the equipment you need and enough time to finish the dish.

Measuring

For many recipes, it is fine to change the amounts of some of the ingredients you are using. You can use more of what you like or what you happen to have plenty of in the cupboard. The more cooking you do, the easier you will find this. If there is the odd disaster along the way, don't worry too much. It happens to the best of cooks!

Other recipes, especially for cakes, need really careful measuring to be successful.

3 Measure out all your ingredients and put them in little bowls or on saucers ready for use. If vegetables need to chopped, or cheese grated, do that now, too.

4 If necessary, turn on the oven so that it will be hot when you are ready for it. It's always worth checking that there isn't anything in it before you switch it on!

5 Work through the recipe step by step. Don't be afraid to ask if you don't understand something.

6 Most important of all, have fun! If you enjoy cooking, you can look forward to a lifetime of healthy, delicious meals and you'll never be short of friends!

If you are measuring small amounts of liquids or flavourings, it is easiest to use measuring spoons. For dry ingredients, the spoon should be level, not heaped, unless the recipe says so.

5ml = 1 teaspoon
10ml = 2 teaspooons
15ml = 1 tablespoon
30ml = 2 tablespoons
45ml = 3 tablespoons

Mashed potatoes

This is a simple recipe that you can eat with lots of different meals. It can also form the basis of fishcakes, shepherd's pie and other dishes. Choose potatoes that are suitable for mashing, not new or small ones.

SERVES 4

You will need
★ 600g potatoes
★ 50g butter
★ 15–30ml milk
★ salt and pepper

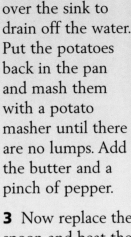

1 Peel the potatoes and cut them into evenly-sized chunks. Place them in a large saucepan, cover them with water, and add 5ml salt. Cover the pan, place it over a high heat, and bring it to the boil. Then turn down the heat and bubble the potatoes gently for about 20–25 minutes, until you can easily push in a sharp knife.

2 Very carefully tip the potatoes into a colander over the sink to drain off the water. Put the potatoes back in the pan and mash them with a potato masher until there are no lumps. Add the butter and a pinch of pepper.

3 Now replace the masher with a wooden spoon and beat the potatoes, gradually adding the milk, until they are creamy.

4 Plain mashed potatoes are great, but you could also add flavourings, such as grated cheese, pesto, wholegrain mustard or horseradish. Or experiment yourself!

Savoury mince

This is a useful basic recipe. It's good on its own, with vegetables or in a baked potato, but it can also be the basis of a cottage pie, spaghetti bolognese and lots of other dishes. You could also use lamb, pork or turkey mince.

SERVES 4

You will need
★ 500g mince
★ 1 large onion, finely chopped
★ 15ml vegetable oil
★ 150ml water
★ 1 beef stock cube
★ salt and pepper
★ 10ml cornflour

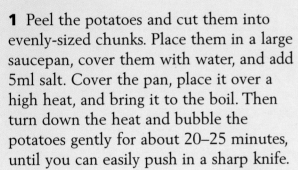

1 Heat the oil in a large saucepan over a medium heat. Add the mince and onion. Prod the mixture with a wooden spoon to mix the onion and meat and to break up the mince as it starts to cook.

2 When the meat is beginning to brown and is in small pieces, add the water and crumble in the stock cube. Stir well and, when the mixture begins to bubble, reduce the heat a little and allow it to simmer gently for 20–30 minutes.

3 Add the salt and pepper to taste. Mix the cornflour with 30ml cold water in a small bowl or cup. Stirring the meat with one hand, pour this mixture in with the other. The gravy will thicken.

Sandwich cake

Once you can make this easy all-in-one recipe, you'll be able to produce a whole range of teatime treats, from buns to birthday cakes. Remember that you need to weigh and measure very carefully when baking.

MAKES 12 BUNS OR
ONE 18CM SANDWICH CAKE

You will need
★ 125g self-raising flour
★ 5ml baking powder
★ 125g soft margarine at room temperature
★ 125g caster sugar
★ 2 large eggs

1 Sieve the flour and baking powder together into a large bowl. Add the margarine, sugar and eggs.

2 With a wooden spoon, gently mix the ingredients together, until you have a smooth and glossy mixture. It's now ready to use in your recipe (see pages 18 and 25).

Melting chocolate

If you can melt chocolate, you can make all sorts of delicious desserts and decorations, but it can be tricky. If you overheat chocolate, it becomes thick and dull and can't be rescued. Here are two ways of making sure this doesn't happen – one using a microwave oven and one using an ordinary hob.

MICROWAVE METHOD

1 Break the chocolate into pieces and put them into a plastic microwave-proof bowl Don't use a glass or china bowl as it may get too hot.

2 Heat the chocolate on medium power in 1-minute bursts. After each minute, stir the chocolate, remembering to take the spoon out when you put the bowl back in the microwave. Stop as soon as the chocolate has no lumps.

HOB METHOD

1 Find a small saucepan and a heatproof bowl that can sit safely in the top of it.

2 Pour water into the saucepan so that it comes about a third of the way up the sides. Make sure that when you replace the bowl, the bottom of it doesn't touch the water. Bring the water to the boil over a high heat and then reduce the heat so that the water bubbles very gently.

3 Break the chocolate into the bowl and carefully (wearing oven gloves) sit it over the water. Keep an eye on the chocolate. It should take between 5 and 15 minutes to melt.